Conductor Kash
and the Prosperity Express

Published through ImaginePublishing.com, 3428 – 99 Street Suite 444, Edmonton, Alberta, Canada, T6E 5X5 www.ImaginePublishing.com
by Shira Enterprises Inc. www.KidzMakeCents.com

First printed in Canada.

Library and Archives Canada Cataloguing in Publication

Deep, Kim, 1967-
    Conductor Kash and the prosperity express : ABCs of prosperity / written by Kim Deep ; illustrated by Jared Robinson.

ISBN 978-1-897409-12-1

    1. Finance, Personal--Juvenile literature. 2. Money--Juvenile literature.
3. Children--Finance, Personal--Juvenile literature.

I. Robinson, Jared, 1979- II. Title. III. Series: Ready-set-grow!
(Chicago, Ill.)

HG179.D432 2008   j332.0240083   C2008-904115-1

**Dedicated to Shelby, Garret, and Amber
who always inspire me to be the best MOM
i can be, and love me even when i get messy!
~Love Mom xoxo**

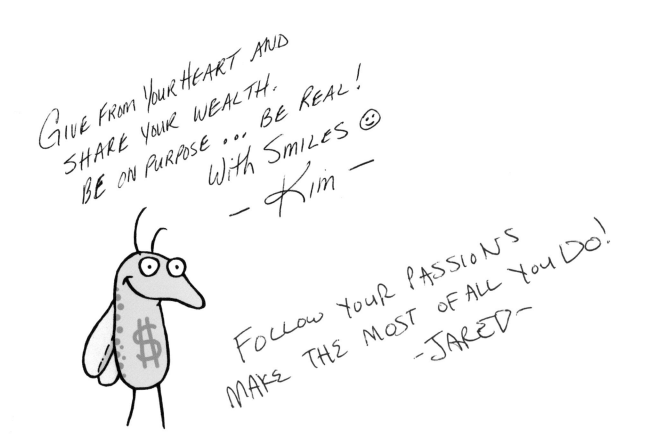

Give from your Heart and
Share your Wealth.
Be on purpose ... Be Real!
With Smiles ☺
— Kim —

Follow your Passions
Make the most of all you Do!
— Jared —

CONDUCTOR KASH
and the Prosperity Express

Written by Kim Deep
Illustrated by Jared Robinson

Conductor Kash tugged on the train whistle.
"Choo-Choose, Choo-Choose!"

SUCCESS is MINE

He said, "Get on board girls and boys.
Let's take a journey.
It's all about financial *Success*,
We can show you how on the Prosperity Express!"

The kids jumped onto the train
without hesitation
Slowly the money train pulled
away from the station

Building speed
and heading up the railway line
It chanted
"Success is Mine, Success is Mine!"

Conductor Kash smiled at each child
Sharing his heart and mission
His laugh and energy filled the air
He said, "Money is one of life's greatest lessons"

We love taking vacations and having fun,
Let's get started at the Prosperity Station.

We like to plan our
holiday trips with care
So that we can get safely
from here to there.

Life is also an adventure
As we go from point A to point Z
Embrace our natural gifts
and fulfill our destiny

One way is to enjoy the journey
and find our niche
Let's create our own *Wealth*
and become very rich

Let's learn about money, it's the way to go
Let's start with A and go with the alphabet flow
Know that awareness, attitude and action are free
Focus your attention and grow your own prosperity tree

A is for *Assets*
that work hard for me
To work smart,
have fun
and make tons of money

C is for *Cash flow* and Choice to pay bills when due
And to give Charity to others, no matter who

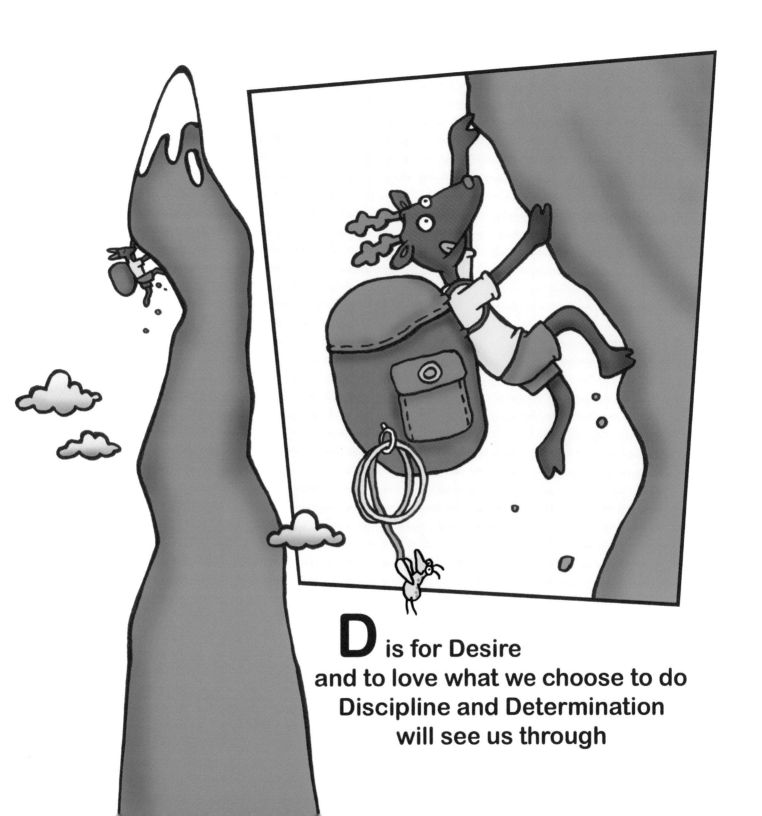

D is for Desire
and to love what we choose to do
Discipline and Determination
will see us through

E is for Expectation, Emotion and Effort to succeed
Creating positive Energy that supports our deeds

F is for *Financial Freedom* and having choice
Have Financial wisdom and a Rolls Royce

H is for *Habits*
that encourage our success
Finding Health and Happiness
and not distress

I is for *Investment* Income to feather our nest
A nest egg of golden eggs is what we like best

J is for Joy that comes
from money and wealth
It makes our lives easier
and promotes good health

K is for Knowledge
to seek more clarity
Knowing what we want
and who to be

L is for the Love of Learning
and Love of Life
Sharing our gifts and talents
to end world strife

M is for Managing our Money with skill and CARE
Knowing what we have and claiming our share

N is for Never Needing anything right now
But *Saving* and planning to get it somehow

O is for Opening our minds and our hearts
Seeing Opportunities that give us a head start

P is for *Prosperity* and *Passive Income* is best
Our money works hard for us while we rest

Q is for Quieting the mind to allow space
The heart and spirit are the creative place

R is for Resources
and financial tools that assist
Recreation and balance
allow us to persist

S is for Systemizing our Savings with CARE
Getting rid of guess work and Saving our share

T is for Trusting
in ourselves and others too
Be who we are
and to ourselves always be True

U is for Using mistakes
to build our success

We only fail when
we quit and not do our best

V is for Valuing ourselves and living our Vision
Earn money to help others and to fulfill our mission

W is for Wealth and balance in life and all we do
Money is about results and a necessity for us too

X

is for Xpressing ourselves
and being heard
Modelling success
and being the lead bird

Y is for the *Yield* or what we earn on our money
Our percentage can be great and sweet as honey

Z is for Zooming into the present to take *Action*
Living in the moment gives the most satisfaction

The Prosperity Express pulled back into the station
The trip was over but lessons not forgotten

Conductor Kash said, "Come back anytime to take a trip
We will travel again to somewhere hip
For learning about money and wealth is really cool
Prosperity is learned just like subjects in school."

MEET THE CREW

CONDUCTOR KASH

**believes in you
with all his heart
You are courageous,
kind and really smart!**

BENJI the BEAVER

works from dusk to dawn
Because his passion
is always number one

BECKY the BIRD

is generous and kind
But she always saves
a penny from every dime

ROZ the RABBIT

likes to take action
Completing a job
gives her great satisfaction

MARCUS the MOOSE

really likes to have fun
Letting it all hang out
and doing lots of recreation

TIMMY the TURTLE

is calm and cool
Setting some goals
and learning at school

MARTY the MONEY-BUG

is smart as can be
Helping you grow
your own Prosperity Tree

Please travel back to the beginning of the book
See if you can find Marty where ever you look
The Money Bug is sometimes shy and hard to find
So look at each page carefully and FOCUS your mind

CAN YOU FIND
MARTY
THE MONEY BUG?

Each time you find Marty, shout really loud
"I caught the Money Bug".
For when you live with heart and play really BIG
Life is more fun and you get back what you give!

Learning the Language of Money

Can you find these words in the book?

Success is wanting what you get

Wealth is having what you want in all areas of life

Focus is putting your attention on what is important to you

Assets are the stuff or things you own that feed you

Business is earning value or money from trading products or services

Cash flow is the money that is left over after expenses are paid

Financial Freedom is having enough passive income to pay for your chosen lifestyle

Habits is doing something over and over again without thinking

Investment is something that you put your money, time or resources into while expecting to get more back in return

Saving is a plan to put money away before you spend it all on piddlyscrap

Prosperity is having an abundance of what is important to you

Passive Income is your money working for you; work once and get paid many times

Yield is money or profit earned on an investment

Action is putting into motion through your own will

Money Wise Quiz

1. Benji the Beaver has a new business.
What is the selling price for a glass of lemonade?

2. How many jars of honey does Timmy the Turtle have ready to sell?

3. How many windows does Roz the Rabbit
have in her apartment building?

4. Becky the Bird is going on vacation.
How many coins and bills does she have saved?

5. Marcus the Moose is a great saver.
How many piles of money does he have?

6. Timmy the Turtle never gives up.
How many nails has he hammered in straight?

7. How many bags of money does Benji the Beaver
have working for him while he sleeps?

8. What is the total number of money bags that the Crew
is loading onto the Prosperity Express train?

9. Is Becky's nest for sale?

10. How many Marty the Money Bugs can you find in the book?

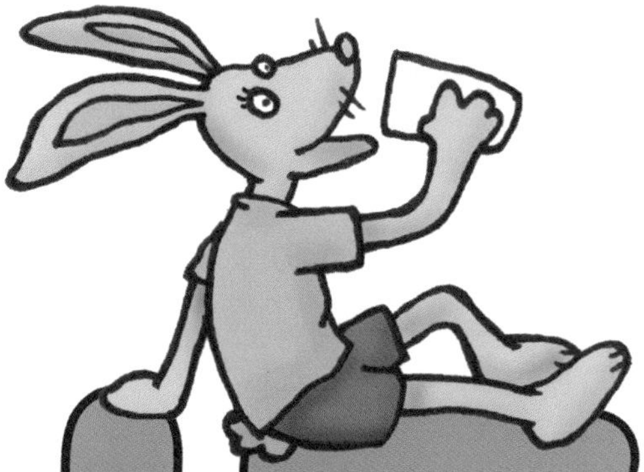

THE END

AUTHOR - KIM DEEP

Kim is a Certified Management Accountant, business coach and trainer with over two decades of experience in the business and finance areas. Kim has worked along side some of the top trainers and coaches in the world. She is well respected for her down-to-earth communication style and her creative and fun approach to helping young kids feel empowered and learn basic money skills. She is also the founder and President of Kidz Make Cents, an organization dedicated to empowering kids to "lead with heart" using financial literacy, communication strategies and leadership skills as fundamental guiding principles. With three children of her own, Amber, Garret and Shelby, Kim is passionate about teaching financial literacy and leadership skills at an early age. As a MOM (Manager of Money) Kim loves working with kids and inspiring them to embrace their natural talents and use all the tools at their disposal to achieve personal success...and to enjoy life in the process! For more information on financial literacy programs, check www.kidzmakecents.com

ILLUSTRATOR - JARED ROBINSON

Jared is an artist in the true sense. Educated and experienced in digital design, videography, illustration, and acrylic painting; he develops each area professionally and creatively. This, mixed with his love and involvement with children, provides the perfect platform to illustrate children's books. He started his own media company, and has since enjoyed the variety of work that comes his way; with projects including the creation of promotional DVD's, coloring contests, art shows, logos, book illustrations, and music videos. He enjoys the outdoors as well, from surfing and snowboarding to camping and caving. Whether it's work or play, Jared likes to live life to the fullest, enjoying every step along the way!

For more work jared has completed, check www.eye-catchers.ca

Printed in the United States
126035LV00001BB